DRAWING ...IS FUN!

You'll be amazed at what you can do!

By Susie Hodge

Susie Hodge

ISBN 1-902731-04-4

First published in 2000 by Writers' Bookshop,
Remus House, Coltsfoot Drive, Woodston,
Peterborough PE2 9JX

© Susie Hodge 2000

DRAWING ...IS FUN!

Introduction

The first drawings we know about were scratched on cave walls about 30 000 years ago. We don't know what started people drawing, but we do know that everyone can learn to draw.

Thousands of years ago in ancient Egypt, artists began training at four years old! When they grew up, they became master artists and trained the next generation.

About this book

This book tells you about how to improve your drawing skills and to develop effective techniques. It gives you advice on various materials and methods that you can use to produce skilful and accurate drawings. And it's full of information and practical tips that many professional artists use all the time.

Without stifling your personality and originality, the book explores ideas and ways of drawing all sorts of things, from animals and trees to people and machines. So whether you're drawing from real life, from photographs or from your imagination, you'll quickly understand how to make your pictures more effective.

You don't have to go through the book chapter by chapter. You can dip in and out as you please. But even if you don't want to draw certain subjects, read everything anyway because each page contains valuable information that will help you in other areas of your drawing.

By the time you finish the book, if you've followed it as it says, you'll be able to draw all sorts of things in all sorts of ways and you'll have developed your own

DRAWING . . . IS FUN!

drawing style. You'll be amazed at how quickly you improve once you start.

Practice!

This might sound boring, but if you're serious about learning to draw (and all artists learn to draw before anything else) then you'll have to practice and keep practicing. Drawing is the base of every artistic expression, from paintings and sculpture, to TV programmes, fashion design and architecture. Even your toothbrush started as a drawing! The world needs people who can draw. So draw as much and as often as you can. But don't spend hours on it if it means you lose the enjoyment. A simple ten-minute sketch that you enjoy is far better than a painstaking picture that you're fed-up with. One thing that all great artists have in common is that they have fun doing it.

And stop saying you can't! You can! The less you think about how you are doing and concentrate more on what you are doing, the better your drawing will be. Be as bold as you dare and be proud of your achievements. Use whatever materials to help you achieve your best work. It's not cheating. So the next time someone says to you 'I couldn't draw a straight line to save my life!' give him or her a ruler.

Everybody can draw!

How you drew when you started school will be different to the way you draw now. Small children see the world in a different way to older children and adults. As you grow older, you start to worry more about whether your drawing is 'correct,' whether it looks like the thing you are trying to draw - like a photo. This is often where you give up, saying:

"There's no point in me trying to draw, it's a gift and I don't have it."

Sound familiar?

But rather than a gift, drawing is a skill which can be learnt. Of course, some artists are geniuses, but most of us can become accurate and accomplished at drawing without that. Everyone can learn to draw. It's simply about learning to look properly and knowing where and how to make the marks. Learning to draw (or to draw better) will boost your creativity and your confidence. Learning to draw properly will show you how much of a gift you really do have! And it's a myth that those who can draw well find it easy. Artists work hard to produce great art, so expect to make a bit of an effort and you'll soon discover your hidden talents!

Magic Drawing

Drawing has always been seen as a mysterious force. Thousands of years ago, it was believed to have magical powers. Animals drawn on cave walls would magically be captured in the next hunt; people who had died would magically step out of their pictures into a life after death.

Well, who knows? But drawing certainly has a lot to answer for. Each

DRAWING . . . IS FUN!

letter of every word you have read so far came from drawings originally. The first writing began as pictures representing sounds. Gradually these evolved into the symbols we read and write with today.

Here are four examples of some early writing:

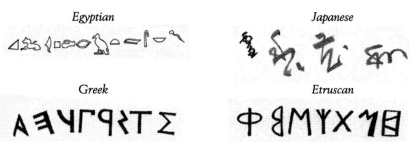

Egyptian

Japanese

Greek

Etruscan

You can see how some of these developed into the writing we use today. Which all adds up to one thing -

If you can write your name, you can draw!

It's true! Writing is just about drawing lines, shapes and dots in the right places - something that most people do automatically. So start exploring drawing right now and design your own name! Draw symbols for each letter, or copy a style of lettering. Try forgetting the letters you know and creating your own. Fill a whole page with ideas -use pencils, pens, felt-tips or pastels - whatever you like. Draw guidelines or doodle freely. You can't go wrong; it's your name!

When you're happy with your name design, make yourself a sign for your bedroom door.

Materials and Equipment

You don't need much to start drawing. You can use a pencil, pen, crayon or chalk on any kind of paper. But some things are useful and will help you to achieve different effects.

Start with what you already have and add to your materials gradually.

Paper can be bought in all shapes, sizes, textures and colours. A pad of cartridge paper is all you need to start, but as your drawing improves, try a wider range of paper. For instance, pen and ink or fineliners work well on smooth-surfaced paper. Pastels and chalks work better on coloured paper with a 'tooth' or texture. Thicker papers can take more pressure than others. Lighter papers are usually cheaper and good for experimenting on.

Pencils are inexpensive and about the easiest things to draw with. Hard pencils are marked with an H - a 4H for example, is harder than a 2H. H pencils make faint, hard lines. They are good for technical drawings, but can be hard to rub out. Soft pencils are marked with a B - standing for black. A 6B for example, is softer than a 3B. B pencils are good for sketching and shading. HB pencils are in the middle.

Pens can also be bought cheaply. Ballpoint pens slide over the paper and can create different textures and tones. You can't shade from dark to light with pen and ink or fineliners but they're good for line drawings. Felt-tips can be thick or thin, in brilliant colours and waterproof or non-waterproof. They are great for drawing, colouring and blending.

Charcoal smudges easily and is good for tonal drawings. Charcoal pencils are less messy and give a sharper line.

DRAWING . . . IS FUN!

Chalk pastels are easily blended. They come in wonderful colours, but start with just a few and see how you like them.

Oil pastels come in bright colours and blend well when you layer them on top of each other.

Coloured pencils or crayons come in different qualities. Buy the best you can afford.

These can be blended and shaded well. If yours are water soluble, colour in as usual then paint with a clean, wet paintbrush. It will turn into a vividly coloured watercolour!

Extra things

As well as all the equipment mentioned so far, you'd find certain other materials useful:

A good quality eraser - the plain white, soft rubber or plastic varieties are best. As well, you might like to try a putty rubber, which can be squashed into any shape you like, and used to lift off mucky or surplus pencil, charcoal or pastel marks. You'll need a craft knife or pencil sharpener and maybe a drawing board. Some kitchen roll or cotton buds are useful for blending charcoal and pastels. And you'll need a ruler for perspective drawing.

Keeping a sketchbook

All artists use sketchbooks. They use them for jotting down visual 'notes' - reminders of things they've seen and been interested in, for trying out new drawing materials and techniques and for developing their drawing style. Sketchbooks, along with pencils, are the basic must-haves of all artists.

You can use a sketchbook to experiment with, for scribbling down ideas, as a visual diary or as a place to store information. If you see something you are interested in when you're out and about, you can make quick sketches to remind yourself of what it looked like later on. You can even use a sketchbook like a scrapbook and stick in photos, postcards, magazine pictures and illustrations that appeal to and inspire you.

It's a good idea to have at least two sketchbooks. Carry a small one around with you wherever you go and keep a larger one at home. Always keep a pen or pencil handy and use your sketchbooks as often as you can. They'll help you to keep in practice.

Buying sketchbooks

You can buy sketchbooks quite cheaply. They come in all sorts of shapes, sizes and thicknesses and with many different qualities of paper. You don't need an expensive one to start with, although check that the paper is not too flimsy. Ringbound sketchbooks are easy to flip over when you've finished a picture or an idea. Some sketchbooks have hard covers that can be useful to lean on; some have pages that can be torn out easily. They all have advantages and disadvantages, so have a look around and see what's available. As you improve, you might want to keep several sketchbooks for different purposes - one as a scrapbook, one for drawing people and another for drawing places and objects perhaps.

Getting started

The drawings you make in your sketchbook should vary from the slightest notes to fairly detailed work. Jot down colour ideas; draw people at the bus stop or out shopping; draw trees and animals, or parts of buildings. Collect details about lighting and colour. Work out compositions - or layouts - of drawings in quick, miniature sketches.

Date all your drawings and keep your sketchbooks. Keep your mistakes as well as your successes. Look back on them to see how you've improved and to inspire you with ideas you might have forgotten.

Draw something in your sketchbook everyday. Try out charcoal, felt-tips, pencils and pens. Get used to how they feel and the effects they make. And keep drawing what you see around you, copying photographs, jotting down ideas.

As you use your sketchbook more, your drawing skills will improve and your confidence will grow. The more you draw, the better you'll become!

First shapes

Most drawings begin as outlines, even though nothing in nature actually has an outline. We recognise things by their shapes and an outline of a shape is one of the clearest ways of representing an object. But some shapes seem quite complicated. How do you get the outline right? And if there is more than one object, all the shapes overlap and the different outlines become confused.

So you need to simplify what you're looking at. Break it down into simple shapes and angles and mark those on your paper. Sounds easy, but at first it can be quite difficult. Usually, when we look at something, our brain tells us what it is - a cup, a hand or whatever. When we try to draw it, we don't draw the object in front of us, but the idea we have in our heads of what it looks like.

Clear your mind. Draw only what you actually see in front of you, not what you think is there. Stop your brain telling you how you think that object looks and see everything with fresh eyes!

Negative space

As well as looking at the positive shapes, train yourself to look at the negative space. For example, the gaps between your fingers, the hole inside a cup handle, the sky around a tree and so on. Drawing outlines becomes easier when you compare all the shapes against each other and against the spaces around them.

DRAWING . . . IS FUN!

To start drawing, use a well-sharpened 2B pencil and a sheet of paper or your sketchbook. Find a simple object, such as a mug, a cup or an apple. Sit comfortably. Remember that an object changes its shape depending on where you look at it from. Look closely at your object and visualise its shape on to your paper. Aim to fill the page. If your lines wobble, correct them or start again. Check and check again, by spending more time looking at the object than at your drawing.

Once you've had a go at an outline drawing of one object, try a small group. Put about three objects together, so that their shapes appear to overlap as you look at them. With a fresh sheet of paper or page of your sketchbook, lightly draw the main shapes. Notice the way the shapes relate to each other - where and how do they overlap? How much larger, taller or wider is one shape from another? What is the proportion of the width to the height? And don't forget the negative spaces - look at the shapes between and behind the objects. If you draw only the negative spaces, you might not have to draw the actual objects at all!

Fun with faces

How did you draw faces when you were little? A circle for the head, two dots for eyes, a line each for the nose and mouth? We instantly recognise that as a face. But real-looking faces are far more interesting to draw and to look at.

Get into the habit of really looking at faces. What shape are the eyes? Where do shadows fall? You'll need your sketchbook or paper and a pencil or charcoal. You're going to draw a real-looking face right now.

Expect to make mistakes. Everyone does. Visit an art gallery to see how many great works have been completely redrawn and painted. Soon you'll be able to draw portraits. But to start with, here are a few important facts.

Heads are round

Even though your paper is flat, remember that the head is three-dimensional. Lightly draw an egg shape, narrow part at the bottom. We all have different shaped faces so you'll probably have to make some adjustments later.

Now let's look at the eyes. They're not at the top of the head, but almost half way down. Leave room above the eyes for lids and brows. Draw curved lids with the iris and pupil between. There's more about drawing features on pages 20 and 21. Don't draw eye outlines heavily. Add a few flicks at the outer corners for eyelashes and more dashes for eyebrows above.

Shadow shapes

Don't draw lines on either side of the nose; draw only the shadow shapes you

DRAWING . . . IS FUN!

can see under the nostrils. The tip or underside of the nose is about half way between the eye and the chin.

Halfway between the end of the nose and the chin is the mouth. Mouths are usually the same length as the distance between the pupils of the eyes. Draw the centre line first. Unless the person is wearing heavy lipliner, the edges of the mouth are just a soft colour change. Show this by shading the top lip. Often the lower lip can be drawn as a shadowed area beneath it.

Ears look like sausage shapes on each side of the face. They stretch from eye level to the bottom of the nose. Draw the outer shape of the hair. Lightly! Look at people's hair. Where does it grow from? Where does the light catch it? Where is it darkest? (More about hair on pages 22 and 23.)

Now put in two lines for the neck, making sure that it's not too thin. Add some shading and there's your face! As you practice, you'll be able to add more shading and details.

Find someone who won't be offended if you practice drawing his or her face. Tell them you are just starting out but with their help you could become a famous portrait artist and they'll be remembered in history.

Perfect profiles

Drawing portraits from the side - profiles - can be fun to do.

First of all, the basic shape of a profile is a circle not an egg shape as a portrait from the front is. There's also more hair on show than on a face seen from the front. Ask someone to model for you. They can sit and read, watch TV or even sleep - it doesn't matter as long as they sit long enough for you to get the proportions right! Sit about 1.5 metres away and in a position where you can see their profile clearly. First, imagine the head as an empty shape and look for the negative space around it. Draw that shape lightly on your paper. Notice that the neck does not go straight down from the bottom of the head, but at an angle. Check that your necks always join the head in the right place at the back.

Mark on a slightly tilted cross as a guideline. Then draw some hair and the chin in more detail. The eye sits on the cross, set back from the nose and looks like a triangle from the side. Work out the angle of the nose by comparing it to other angles on the face. Does it curve? Is it long or short? Draw the shape beneath the nostrils. Continue up to where the nose becomes the forehead, and then move down to where it joins the lips and then the chin. Check to see whether your model's chin sticks out or recedes.

Details

The eyeball is just that - a round ball behind the lids. The lids follow the eye's rounded shape and are a layer

DRAWING . . . IS FUN!

thicker than the eye itself. Draw the white of the eye to get the iris shape right rather than trying to draw the coloured part straight away. These are all ways to make you draw what is actually there and to stop your brain taking over and telling you what it thinks is there!

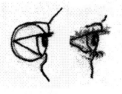

For any shape you find hard to draw, stop looking at it and draw the negative space next to it.

When you're drawing the lips, notice where they come compared to the tip of the nose and the chin. Where lips meet in the centre, the line is a) curved, not straight and b) looks darker than the rest, so needs shading or colouring.

The top of the ear is parallel to the top of the eye, where the guidelines cross. The bottom of the ear is usually parallel to the bottom of the nose. Add eyelashes; shade the eyes, leaving a white highlight. Shade gently around the nose, the edges of the face and under the chin. Shade the hair, leaving areas for shine and add some darker lines for definition.

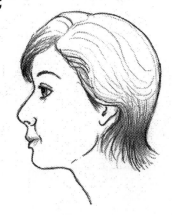

Fun with features

So now you can draw faces from different angles. But to draw recognisable portraits, you need to be able to draw individual-looking features. Apart from face-shape and hair, the features are the most distinctive characteristics of all.

Eyes

 Always remember to position the eyes about halfway down the head.

Eyes vary in shape, size and colour. Look at lots of people's eyes - old, young, behind glasses, with make-up. Really look at the shapes. Notice how the top lid curves more than the bottom lid. Some lids are heavy, some slope downwardly and some protrude. To draw eyes from the front, draw the ball shape lightly, add curved eyelids and shade one side of the entire eye gently. As with the profile eye, draw the shapes of the white part of the eye to get the iris right. This shape is also slightly different in everybody. Draw a small triangle shape in the inner corners. Eyelashes don't grow from the inner corners of the eye, so don't draw them all the way round.

The distance between two eyes is about one eye's width. Draw surprised eyes wide open. The only time you can see the whites around the iris. Smiling eyes have crinkly lines at the corners. Angry eyes have frown lines in between; with eyebrows like a 'v'. Eyebrows vary too. Some are arched, some straight. Draw small feathery strokes in the direction they grow.

DRAWING . . . IS FUN!

Mouths

Mouths curve slightly. Start drawing them with the line between the lips. This always looks dark. Lightly draw the outline of the upper and lower lips. Lightly shade the shadowed areas, leaving the lightest parts unshaded. The top lip usually looks darker than the bottom lip. Add a shadow under the bottom lip. For a smiling mouth - don't draw every tooth, just a general shape.

Babies and little children have small, pouty lips. Old people have thinner, lined lips. Men's lips are usually longer, narrower and paler than women's - whose lips are fuller, smaller and often look darker than men's.

Ears and noses

Ears are interesting! Forget what they are and draw what you see! Draw your friends' and families' ears when they're not looking. Look at them from the front (some stick out more) and from full view. Draw the outline shape first, and then shade the ear-hole. Draw the curling shapes and shadows.

Noses are curved wedge-shapes that jut out. Don't draw an outline, but use light and shadow to show the form. Leave the light parts white and shade in the shadowed areas. There is usually a dark shadow beneath the nose - sometimes you can see the nostrils and sometimes you can't. Shade either side of the nose between the eyes.

Drawing hair and caricatures

Although it's made up of lines, don't draw each single hair or you'll never finish your picture! Look for the light and shade - where does the hair shine? Is it darkest at the roots or at the ends? See all the hair as one shape. (Draw the negative space). Add a few lines here and there for definition. Use a soft pencil or a range of pencils (2B is good, but add a 3B or 4B for more depth of shading as well).

Now consider the overall texture. Is it curly? Straight? Plaited? Short? Long? Thinning? Each style or hair type needs different drawing techniques. Hair reflects light and has several other tones in it as well.

Beards and moustaches

Study men's beards and moustaches! See how they grow and where they come from on the face. Like eyebrows, draw them with light, feathery strokes in the direction of growth. Shade the darker areas and leave some highlights untouched.

Glasses

If you're drawing someone who's wearing glasses, before you draw the glasses, draw the negative space around them. This will stop you drawing all the details of the glasses but probably in the wrong proportions! When you've drawn the negative space, you can fill in things like hinges and patterns on the frame.

DRAWING . . . IS FUN!

Caricatures

Whether you're drawing portraits from a live model or a photograph, you can turn your drawings into individual caricatures. You might find you have a real 'knack' for these - and you'll be in demand from friends and family to draw caricatures of everyone! To start, find one prominent or obvious feature and emphasise it as you draw. Don't use as much shading as you would on your usual drawings and try to keep the whole thing simple. Caricatures are good in black and white and also with some coloured pencil shading.

Squint your eyes at the object you are looking at, in this case, hair. By half-closing your eyes, you will block out most of the colour and will see the light and dark only. Leave the highlights unshaded and shade the darkest tones with your softest pencil. Notice how the hair grows or hangs and follows the shape of the head in different places. Dark hair should not be drawn as a dark blob, but leave highlights where the light shines and reflects. In the same way, fair hair shouldn't be left as just an outline. Add a few lines in the direction the hair is laying and to mark the darker tones. Hairstyles, such as ponytails, buns and so on, must all be drawn as a shape first. Then add the details with lines in the direction the hair grows, twists or is tied.

Self-portrait

A good way to learn more about drawing is to set up a mirror and draw yourself. You can do this whenever you like. Artists throughout the ages have drawn themselves to develop their skills.

As with any drawing from observation, you need to spend about 60% of your time looking and 40% of your time drawing.

Rembrandt van Rijn (1606-69) and Vincent van Gogh (1834-90) painted more self-portraits than any other famous artists. They showed how they aged and how they felt at the time.

Try out different poses and different lighting. Consider eye level. Will you look up or down in your portrait? Now look closely at your face as if you hadn't seen it before. What shape are your eyes? Do you have thin lips or full? Change expressions. How do your features change shape?

Pastel portraits

Pastels are great for portraits. Unlike pencils, smudging with your fingers can shade them. Try blues, greens and purples instead of black for shadows.

Really look at what you're drawing and only use the colours you can see. For example, you might imagine your lips as red, but they're more likely to be a deeper skin colour. And have you noticed how many colours there are in your eyes?

If you're quite pleased with your portrait, make a frame out of card and give it to someone like your gran or your teacher - well, someone who'll admire it anyway!

Rest your paper or sketchbook on a board next to the mirror you are looking in so you don't have to move your head too much from your reflection to your drawing. Start by lightly sketching an egg shape for your face. Make sure the neck is not too thin. Mark a cross as guidelines for the facial features. Next, draw a line halfway between the horizontal 'eyeline' and the chin to mark the tip of the nose. Another line between the nose and the chin marks where the mouth will be. Study your features closely again in the mirror. Copy them, shape for shape. Go carefully. Do your eyes slant up or down? Most people draw eyes and lips with strong outlines, but use gentle shading instead of solid lines unless you're wearing heavy eye and lipliner! And don't forget eyebrows - they can change your whole character. Are yours straight or arched? How wide is your nose? Can you see your nostrils? Will you smile or not? Draw your chin more carefully and don't add every spot or freckle!
Draw the whole shape of your hair, and then add details. Shade with light and dark strokes in the direction it hangs or is tied. Leave highlights unshaded.

Measurements

To get the scale and proportion right, most artists use a system for measuring. It's easiest if you draw the size you see - called 'sight-size.'

You can easily check what sight-size is by placing an object, such as a piece of fruit, on a table and holding up a sketchbook in front of it. (Between you and the object). Close one eye and make two marks on the paper, one for each side of the object. The marks will be sight-size.

Proportions

Sometimes the object will have to be drawn much smaller or bigger than it really is. There's a simple measuring technique to get the proportions right. All you need is a pencil.

First of all, sit up straight. If you have a back to your chair, press your back against it. Now hold up the pencil at arm's length (keep your arm straight and fully outstretched). Close one eye. Align the top of the pencil with the top of the object and slide your thumb down until it reaches the bottom of the object. Hold your thumb there, bring the pencil back to your paper and mark the top and bottom of your object on the paper. Do this over and again - horizontally, diagonally and for negative as well as positive distances. You will build up a series of little marks all over your page, showing measurements in proportion.

By taking these measurements, the size of your drawing will be sight size. To work larger, say, twice the size, double the measurements. Beginners often draw tiny pictures because they think this will be easier, but in actual fact, a larger drawing gives you more freedom and is easier to draw.

Ellipses

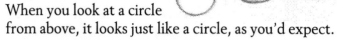

When you look at a circle from above, it looks just like a circle, as you'd expect.

When you look at it from a different angle, it becomes squashed into an ellipse. A common mistake when drawing ellipses is to give them 'corners' which they shouldn't have.

Practice drawing ellipses - turn some of them into cups, bottles, cans and jugs. A simple guideline for an ellipse is a cross. Join the ellipse evenly around each quarter.

For whatever you're drawing, mark on the highest and lowest points and draw a rough overall shape lightly. You can correct any parts if necessary before firming up the lines. And constantly measure and compare the size of one thing to another as you draw. Soon you'll become such an expert that you won't need to measure quite so precisely.

Never alter the distance between your arm, eye and the object you are drawing, so keep your back and arm straight each time.

Tone

Outlines describe the shape of an object and tone describes its form. What's the difference? Well, the shape is the flat shape; the form is the 3D shape. Without touching something, we know its form because we see light and shade on it. This is tone. Tone will make your pictures look 3D. It will help to give your drawings definition and it will set you apart from beginners. By looking through half-closed eyes, detail and colour disappear and tone can be seen more easily. A common mistake is to show tone too lightly. If you look at an object, say a tree, notice how dark the dark tones are. Most of the time, the darkest tones are almost black.

A tonal scale

This is quite a fun exercise and useful for practicing 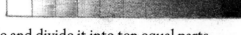 shading. Draw a long rectangle and divide it into ten equal parts. With a soft pencil, shade from white to black, gradually and evenly increasing the intensity of the shading.

You can make a tonal scale with any other medium - ballpoint pens, pastels, coloured pencils and so on, but things like felt-tips and fineliners will not blend. You will have to use other techniques.

Blended shading is when you colour evenly from dark to light as you did in the tonal scale and for small areas on the self-portrait. Don't smudge, but use gentle pressure to build up gradual changes in tone. Leave highlights white.

DRAWING . . . IS FUN!

Stippling is dotting. The closer together you draw the dots, the darker the tone, the further apart the dots, the lighter the tone.

    Hatching is a series of parallel lines. The closer together you draw the lines, the darker the tones. If you criss-cross the lines, this is called cross-hatching. Again, if you draw the cross-hatching close together, you will show darker shadows.

Try a mix of both stippling and cross-hatching.

Putting it all together

Starting a drawing can be a bit daunting. But now you know the basics of drawing shapes and outlines and getting proportions right, find an object or group of objects and arrange them in front of you. Draw it lightly and build up shade with light, almost feathery strokes. Keep looking at your subject while you work. If you make a mistake, don't rush to rub it out. New lines or areas of tone can cover mistakes. If you over shade, use a rubber to pick out the white highlights, or to 'lift' some of the areas that are too dark.

Notice where the light comes from, sometimes it will come from several different sources, which will affect the shading. And notice the cast shadows under and around each object you draw.

Texture and pattern

The texture or feel of an object - rough, smooth, soft, spiky - and the surface appearance of patterns all add to the look of things. Sometimes you draw these without realising and sometimes you're not sure how to draw them or whether they'll spoil what you've already drawn.

Often, showing texture helps a picture. Details of texture and pattern in the foreground of a scene with fewer details in the background make quite a dramatic contrast, like some photographs. Texture and pattern on animal drawings add a realistic touch to the picture.

Showing the feel of things

Start with something simple like a leaf. Look closely and notice all the little veins. Try drawing it with pencil, lightly marking on the pattern of the veins, then blend and shade the dark and light parts. Next, try using pen and ink or a fineliner. You won't be able to blend, but draw delicate lines with some cross-hatching or stippling. Use felt-tips or oil pastels for a third drawing, either leaving the veins white or scratching them out with a pointed object (a hairpin or cocktail stick is fine).

You can do the same with flowers and petals, fur and feathers - anything you like the look of. Try out very soft pencils or charcoal. Use short marks for short fur, grass or tufts of a brush and long strokes for long fur, feathers and so on. Before you start, ask yourself how you could do it best. You'll usually be able to tell whether

DRAWING . . . IS FUN!

stippling or jagged marks, for example are the best techniques to show the right 'feel'.

It's not necessary to put in every mark - every stone on the beach or blade of grass for example. In fact, too much could ruin a good drawing. Just a general idea of shape and tone is often better than too much. For example, don't try to draw every leaf on a tree.

Pattern

Look for patterns in everything you draw, they will help you to build up arrangements and shapes of lines.

Manmade objects such as cars, aeroplanes, boats and houses are designed to have shapes and patterns. Natural objects, such as flowers or rocks have other kinds of patterns. And things like water and the sky reflect, drift or flow in fascinating moving patterns.

You can use patterns and textures from around you as the basis for a design, for a whole picture or for parts of a drawing. They will add to the look of your work, making it more interesting and creating moods.

Use smooth, horizontal patterns for calm pictures or short, sharp diagonal patterns for lively-looking pictures. Backgrounds can be used to change the mood of almost any picture.

Composition

Composition is the layout, design or arrangement of a picture. It's often forgotten but it's one of the most important stages of a drawing. So always plan your pictures before you start. A good way of doing this, is with 'thumbnail sketches'.

Draw four to six small rectangles. They don't have to be literally the size of your thumbnail, but keep them small! Now sketch rough outlines of what you intend to draw, working out what will look best. There are no real rules for good composition but your sense of design will develop as your drawing improves. Every picture needs a 'focal point' - one main area of interest. This is usually in the top or bottom, left or right third of the picture. Too much in your picture will clutter it. On the other hand, too much space round the edges can be dull and the subject will appear to 'float'.

Picture shape and viewpoint

Pictures can be any size and shape but they will also depend upon the subject you are drawing. Landscapes usually fit best into a shape, which is wider than it is tall. Portraits are best in a tall shape. For this reason, paper is described as either 'landscape' or portrait' depending on which way round it is. Also, you need to consider your viewpoint. Looking up at or down on your subject changes the mood. It might be calm or dramatic, depending on your viewpoint.

DRAWING . . . IS FUN!

Our eyes are drawn into a well-composed picture. Comics and magazines are designed to lead your eyes around the page. You need to do the same with your drawings. Be careful not to include things that lead the eye out of it, for example, a path leading away. And don't cut a picture in half with a line going right through it.

Royalty has traditionally been painted from a low viewpoint so that they appear powerfully high. But Charles I was very short, so Sir Anthony van Dyck (1599-1641) painted him sitting on a horse!

Using a viewfinder

Composition is not only about where to place your subject on the paper, but also how large it should be and what else to include. Looking through a viewfinder helps because it shows you instantly how the picture might look. A viewfinder is a frame that you hold up in front of whatever you are drawing so you can see the composition. You can make a viewfinder by cutting a rectangle out of a postcard or stiff paper. Or cut two L-shaped pieces of card, so you can adjust the frame size. Move the viewfinder around until you're happy with the composition you can see - and then draw it!

Still life

Still life is a group of objects that you arrange to draw.
Almost anything makes a good subject for a still life
drawing. You may find an interesting arrangement of
objects or an unusual subject by accident, such as a
group of shells, a bowl of fruit or a pair of trainers.

To arrange a still life, start with a theme such as food
and then choose objects which relate to it. An
arrangement of jewellery, musical instruments or
sports equipment could make a good composition.

Setting up a still life

The arrangement of the objects is important. Don't cram in too
much - five is about enough. They need to look balanced, not too
squashed together or spaced apart, but with some overlap. Keep the
background bare at first or scrunch up a piece of fabric and use the
pattern as your backdrop. Think about textures, patterns and
contrasts. Shiny and dull objects rough and smooth, tall and small. It
all helps to make an interesting final picture.

Use the thumbnail technique or a viewfinder until you find a
composition that you like. Remember that the edges of
the picture are important too.

Lighting

Try different lighting on your arrangement.
Perhaps use an overhead light or a reading
or desk lamp to one side. The shadows
and highlights show the shape and form
of the objects, so use your shading

DRAWING . . . IS FUN!

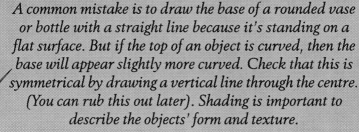

skills. Don't light the group from behind or you'll be drawing it in deep shadow. Lighting from the front can look harsh and shows hardly any tone. Experiment with daylight and electric light for different atmospheres.

Be confident about drawing your still life. Begin by studying the shapes. Then with a soft pencil, make a series of little lines to mark the scale of the arrangement on your paper. Start with the largest object and use it to measure the scale of the other objects around it. A lot of what you see can be simplified into a series of basic shapes, such as cubes and spheres. And look for the negative space - the shapes between objects. You can build up the outline of an object by drawing the space around it. Check the proportions by measuring with a straight-arm and back and see the tone by half closing your eyes.

A common mistake is to draw the base of a rounded vase or bottle with a straight line because it's standing on a flat surface. But if the top of an object is curved, then the base will appear slightly more curved. Check that this is symmetrical by drawing a vertical line through the centre. (You can rub this out later). Shading is important to describe the objects' form and texture.

Perspective

Perspective is a way of drawing, which makes things look 3D on a flat surface. With linear perspective, you use lines to do this. It probably sounds more difficult than it is, but once you know what to do, it's quite easy. Put simply, objects such as trees which you know are about the same size appear smaller the further away they are. Make a note of the rules of perspective and how it works, perhaps in the back of a sketchbook. Once you've got the idea, you won't need to worry about it too much, you'll do it automatically. Perspective is useful for checking drawings to make sure they are correct.

Vanishing points and eye level

The basic rules of perspective are quite simple. If you walk down a straight road, the two sides will seem to meet in the distance. The place where they seem to meet is called the 'vanishing point.' Vanishing points are always on the horizon and this is always at your eye level. The horizon is where the sky appears to meet the ground. If you are tall or high up, your eye level will be higher and so will the horizon and vanishing point. If you are small or low down, your eye level will be lower and so will the horizon and vanishing point.

To find your eye level and the vanishing point, you can try this:

Rest your sketchbook horizontally on the bridge of y o u r nose. Everything you see just above this will be at your eye level. Somewhere on this line - depending in which direction you are looking - will be the vanishing point. One of the main rules of linear perspective is that all receding (going away from you) horizontal lines above your eye level appear to travel down towards it and

DRAWING . . . IS FUN!

all receding horizontal lines below your eye level appear to travel up towards it.

If you draw some guidelines using these rules, the closer an object is to you, the larger it will appear to be. The further away an object is, the smaller it will appear to be.

In the fifteenth century, people seeing a picture drawn using perspective rules for the first time were shocked. They believed the artist had knocked a hole in the wall, as the picture appeared to have such realistic depth.

Design your own room using perspective techniques. Draw a rectangle then draw a smaller one inside it. This is your back wall. Mark on a dot at your eye level for the vanishing point and using a ruler like a pivot, draw furniture, doors and windows. Add details such as skirting boards, lamps and curtains. Colour in with your favourite colours.

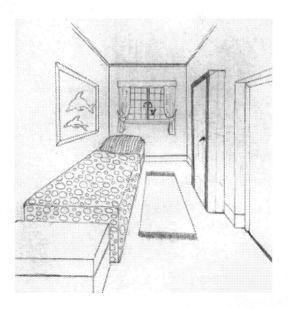

More perspective

Just a bit more about perspective! The methods on the last two pages deal with one vanishing point. This is usually when something is seen from the front and it's called one-point perspective. But mostly we view objects from angles where you can see more than one side. Each side points in different directions and appears to get smaller towards those directions. This is called two-point perspective. For example, if you are drawing a house with a corner facing you, the walls on either side of the corner will appear to go towards opposite vanishing points.

Use the edges of your paper to work out angles. Anything horizontal or vertical should be parallel to the paper's edges. All other angles can be worked out from that. Buildings begin as simple box shapes. Practice drawing boxes from various angles and turn them into buildings. Then add windows, chimneys, doors, roofs, gardens and other details as you did with your room design. You can draw interior or exterior views using this method. Decide where the light is coming from and shade the opposite side darker. This all helps to give the illusion of a 3D image.

If you're drawing from your imagination so can't use any measuring techniques, you can still use perspective to work out scale. For instance, doors must be big enough for people to pass through, cars are wider but lower than doors and streetlights are very tall!

DRAWING . . . IS FUN!

Two vanishing points

A common mistake is to always put the vanishing points within the picture area, when often they're quite a way out. You can tell if you've made this mistake because all the angles will look far too exaggerated. When this happens, put your paper or sketchbook on a larger piece of scrap paper and mark the vanishing points on that. Keep checking vanishing points as you draw. Remember that vanishing points are always on the horizon.

Aerial or atmospheric perspective

As well as objects appearing smaller in the distance, the colours and tones we can see are lessened by the atmosphere over large distances. Colours and details fade the further away they are. Look out of a window and see how everything blurs and becomes blue or purple in the distance. This is called atmospheric or aerial perspective and if you're working in colour, it gives the look of depth and space in your picture. If you're working in one colour only, strong, dark marks separate the foreground from the softer lines of the background.

But above all, perspective is only a guide. Once you've understood and practiced it, you will develop 'visual perspective' - an understanding of how to draw a 3D image on a 2D surface.

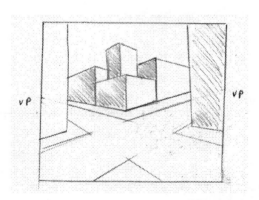

Trees

Trees are fun to draw. They show all the seasons and add richness to pictures. Group them together in landscapes - look for the main patterns and shapes. Not all trees are the same height or the same shape and they add interest to your drawings. Get into the habit of looking at different trees and drawing them in your sketchbook. Draw them from a distance and do some detailed close-up studies of leaves and bark. Most kinds of bark become rougher with age. And leaf shapes vary a lot.

Whatever the season, branches always take up a great amount of space. Start with a light outline. Then look for where the light falls, where shadows are cast and how twigs emerge from the branches. Sketch in the shapes and shade the dark areas.

Do your trees look like lollipops? If they do, you haven't looked properly! Look carefully at the proportions and shapes, but you don't have to include every leaf and bud. Work broadly and build up the overall shape of the tree, breaking the larger shapes into smaller ones as you go.

Roots and branches

Remember that all trees have roots. Show that they g r o w out of the ground and are not just standing on it. Trees grow upwards towards the light, but not all are completely straight. Look for spaces between branches, which let light through and never draw what you can't see - those branches, for example, which are hidden by overhanging leaves.

DRAWING . . . IS FUN!

Use scribbly lines to show the mass of the leaves. Just scribble away, with more scribbles in darker areas. This can look more effective than too many dashes and dots.

Different shapes

Different varieties of trees have different shapes. Some have slim, smooth trunks and dainty, delicately cascading leaves. Some have sturdy, gnarled trunks and large, bunchy leaves.

The seasons

Bare winter trees are a mesh of criss-crossed branches and twigs with lots of spaces in between. Concentrate on the main branches and general shape. Trying to draw every twig will just look messy. In the summer, the leaves are lush and dense. The shape of each tree becomes more bulky. In spring, some trees produce blossom and in autumn, many trees shed their leaves, partially exposing their branches.

Keep in mind where the light's coming from - the leaves might cast shadows on the branches and the bark will look darker in some places. Notice that some leaves look practically black while others, in direct light, appear almost white.

When putting trees in a picture, draw some larger with more details near the front and some smaller and less detailed in the distance.

People

Drawing people is easier than you might think! You just need to look closely at your subject and draw what you see, not your idea of what it looks like. Don't worry if you can't get people to look recognisable at first, it becomes easier with practice. Concentrate on size, positions and proportions.

Copying photographs or using your imagination can be helpful and fun, but for best results you should draw from life. So take your sketchbook everywhere and keep drawing!

Try drawing stick people first. These are fun and quite easy. They'll help you to get started. Include a line each for the shoulders and hips. Fatten the limbs and body with sausage-shapes or cylinders; add hair and some clothing.

Proportion and structure

As with portraits, there are some proportions that are helpful to know. They'll help you to get different parts of the body looking right and in proportion to each other. Although people vary in size and shape, an average adult's height is about seven to eight head lengths. In babies the body is about four head lengths, toddlers are about five head lengths tall and older children are about six head lengths.

When the arms are outstretched, the length from the fingertips of one hand to the fingertips of the other hand is equal to the height of the body. The elbow comes about halfway down the arm and is waist-level. When arms hang down at the sides, the tips of the fingers reach down to halfway between the hips and the knees. Legs are about half the length of the body. Knees are about halfway down the legs.

Leonardo da Vinci (1452-1519) often copied dead bodies when he wanted to draw real-looking people. He 'borrowed' bodies from a local hospital but he got into serious trouble once for taking an important person's body!

Don't worry about drawing details like hands, faces or feet at this stage. Keep to the essentials.

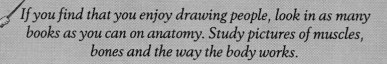

If you find that you enjoy drawing people, look in as many books as you can on anatomy. Study pictures of muscles, bones and the way the body works.

Ask your family or friends to pose for you. It's fine if they sit or stand in a comfortable position, such as watching TV, on the phone, ironing or cooking. Look carefully at them and at the negative spaces around them. With a soft pencil, lightly draw the main shapes. Keep comparing shapes and angles as you draw. For example, is the toe in line with the ear? Does the elbow make a triangular space against the body? Quick sketches like this will give you more confidence to tackle a more detailed drawing.

More people

The human body comes in many different shapes and sizes. Some people are short, some fat, some tall and some thin. But no matter what shape they are, the proportions of the body are nearly always about the same.

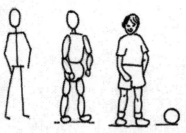

Now you've had a go at sketching some people and you've looked at the main proportions, it's time to look at how to draw it more convincingly. As well as accurate shapes, you need to make the joints bend in the correct way, to shade folds in clothes and to show the balance in weight. This might all sound daunting, but once again, it's not as hard as it sounds.

Constructing the figure

We all change shape as we move. So do our clothes. Some joints can move a lot, whilst others can barely bend. If you find the pose you are drawing confusing, sit or stand in the same position yourself. This will help you to understand just how far and in what direction arms and legs bend, bodies twist and where the weight is distributed.

Always go back to drawing the person as one of your stick/sausage-shaped figures. This simple method will mean that you won't worry about details or accuracy. You can use your stick people as a guide for more precise people drawings.

There are some more details worth remembering as you progress. The head forms a triangle shape with the shoulders. The neck doesn't go straight up, but is set slightly forward on top of sloping

DRAWING . . . IS FUN!

shoulders. Feet are wedge shapes - wider at the toes than at the heel. And study how the body changes in different positions. Don't forget which ways the legs, neck and arms can bend and twist.

Drawing clothes

Although some clothes are more bulky than others, they usually follow the shape of the body. So if you draw them correctly they can help you to make the figure look rounded. For instance, sleeves wrap around the arms and collars curve round the neck. Hats and scarves bend round the head and neck.

Sketch the positions of folds and creases lightly. Notice where the dark tones are and shade them carefully. This also helps to make the body look solid. Shadows form where folds dip in and highlights are where the light falls.

Patterns on clothing help too. By drawing where they bend or meet, you will show how the body bends and twists underneath.

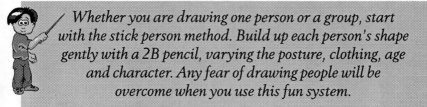

Whether you are drawing one person or a group, start with the stick person method. Build up each person's shape gently with a 2B pencil, varying the posture, clothing, age and character. Any fear of drawing people will be overcome when you use this fun system.

People in action

Once you have had a go at drawing people sitting or standing still, draw some moving! Movements happen too fast for you to be able to draw everything as it happens so you'll need to memorize a certain amount of what you see and add it to your drawing later. Understanding how people move will help you to draw them better. So watch people moving - walking upstairs, getting on buses, eating, drinking, chatting. Notice - and draw - the positions of different parts of bodies as they move. Look at arms, shoulders, heads, legs and so on. Study photographs of moving people too. Then sketch them, over and again in your sketchbook. The only way to become relaxed about this is to keep practicing! Train yourself to see all figures as simple shapes and concentrate on those shapes. Don't worry about mistakes - just keep drawing! Try using pencil, felt-tips, ballpoint pens and chalk pastels. Each is quick and easy to use and each gives a different effect. And don't worry about neatness. Rough sketches often give a better effect than detailed drawings.

Balance

Notice how the balance of the body changes when it moves. Arms swing forward, waists twist, hips tilt. Even if you can't see it from the angle you are drawing, the first part of the body you should think about is the spine. Is it curved, arched or straight? It's important to know what the spine's doing as it sets the balance for the rest of the body. Next, look for the angle of the shoulders and hips. They usually tilt in opposite directions. When you've established spine, hips and shoulders, you can add the limbs. The more you draw, the more you'll recognise how figures shift their weight and hold their balance.

The actions you draw needn't be dramatic. But be aware of how the shapes of bodies change when they move, even slightly. And watch for differences between people. For example, most women's arms hang closer to their bodies than men's and children move more than adults. Whilst you're drawing, constantly compare and contrast the positions of body parts. For example is the left foot in line with the top of the head?

Clothing can help to emphasize movement. It billows out behind the body, flowing in the direction it moves. Hair has the same effect.

Groups of people

Figures in a group interact and overlap. Think of footballers or people talking. Draw these groups, gradually building on the simple stick people technique. Concentrate on general shapes and leave out details. If you're drawing from watching clusters of people, quickly block in the main shapes of the group before they move and the shape changes.

Hands and feet

Now you know how to draw people, it's time to look at some details. Hands can be very expressive and they can strengthen the mood of a drawing.

For a start, hands and feet are larger than you think! Hold your hand over your face with your fingers stretched. It's about as long as the distance from your hairline to your chin! But a common early mistake is to draw hands much too small.

Hands might seem difficult because they are a funny shape. Study them to understand the proportions. There are three main shapes: the palm, the fingers and the thumb. Remember that fingers have three joints and thumbs have two. Start practicing by drawing round your own hand. Take your hand away and draw in the nails and knuckles. Then try a freehand sketch of it. Draw a circle for the palm and add on the fingers. Look for the negative space between fingers and around joints. Notice as well how each finger points in a different direction.

Shapes

Practise drawing your hand or a friend's hand in various poses. Draw as many different hands as you can. Stop thinking it's a hand and only draw the shapes you see in front of you. As with everything else you've drawn so far, look for simple shapes and measurements and draw them lightly first. Note that if the hands and fingers make a rectangle, then the thumb comes from the bottom corner. And that the length of the fingers are about the same length as the palm.

Now let's consider feet. You might think you'll rarely draw bare feet, but you need to know what they look like so that you can draw shoes around them. Try copying your feet from above, from their reflection in a mirror or by taking photographs. It's not so easy to copy your own feet as it is with your hand! Ask your friends and family if you can draw their feet.

Your foot is the same length as the inside of your elbow to your wrist, which is also slightly more than the length of your head. (Don't try measuring this with your own head and foot!)

As with everything else you draw, see feet as simple shapes, noting where the widest and narrowest parts are. Draw the main shapes before adding detail. Seen sideways, the foot is a wedge-shape. The anklebone is in the middle of the ankle and the top of the foot is curved. From the front the inside anklebone is higher than the outside anklebone and the foot looks shorter and wider than it does from the side. (This is to do with perspective). The big toe has only one joint, but the other toes have two.

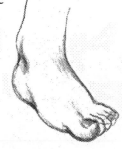

Trains and planes

Using the methods you have learnt so far, try some machines. You might think that trains and planes are difficult, but they needn't be. The usual method applies: stop thinking what it is and draw what you see. If you are drawing from your imagination, draw the basic shapes and add details later.

Draw trains on their own or as a background to another picture. Draw them to look realistic or add you own individual touches. Use perspective and add shading to make them look 3D.

Include lots of detail or draw them as if they are going at high speed, with few details and dashes of coloured lines in the direction they are moving. As trains are made up of box shapes, draw several long boxes using one-point perspective. (Your vanishing point doesn't have to be in the middle of the page). As with a house drawn in this way, add details, such as doors and windows after you've got the shape right. In this way, you can draw trains from the side, coming towards you or going away from you. Or try drawing two snaking lines, going closer together into the distance. Divide this snake into carriages and add details as before.

The next time you see a train, look at it carefully. Notice things like lettering or patterns, the shape of the windows, the curve of the roof, the wheels and what the front looks like.

DRAWING . . . IS FUN!

Old steam trains are fun to draw too. Start with a horizontal cylinder with a box on it. Draw ovals for wheels if you're looking at it from the front, circles if you're looking at it from the side. Add a smaller cylinder chimney on the large cylinder and add details.

The great artist J. M. W. Turner (1775-1851) painted a picture of a steam train using few details and a lot of misty looking steam plus some dark shapes. He said that before he painted it, he stuck his head out of a train speeding towards another so that he could get the effect just right.

Planes

These aren't quite so 'boxy' as trains. The main body of planes and jets is like a long, squashed oval. Again, you need to use perspective when you add on the wings, as these will appear smaller in the distance. Viewed from the front, a plane or jet will look wide, getting smaller towards the back. Viewed from beneath (or above) it will look more streamlined and probably the same on each side. Add details like windows and doors. Show shine by colouring everything in but leaving streaks of white along the length of the plane. Put a squiggle of blue in each window.

Cars, bikes and boats

As with trains and planes, cars, bikes and boats can be drawn easily using some of the techniques you've learnt so far.

Cars are quite boxy, so they can be drawn using perspective techniques. Think of a flattish box with four circles in each corner. Add a smaller box on top. You can alter the proportions to make a small rounded car, a slimline sports car or a square four-wheel drive car. Wheels seen from the side look oval. And use shading for that solid and shiny look. Even if you get the shape right, you need to include shadows and shine lines. When you've drawn a car or several cars you're pleased with, try shading them with soft-pencils or colouring them with felt-tips, pastels or coloured pencils. Watercolour pencils work well. For a look of movement, add short dashes in a particular direction.

It only takes a slight change of shape to make a lorry or bus, but make sure that the cab part is separate from the main part of the van. Next time you're in a car or bus, study vans, lorries and buses for those extra details, such as number plates and shapes of windows.

Bikes

Pushbikes have two equal-sized wheels. The frame is roughly an M shape with the top and left-hand lower parts joined. Add the seat or draw a person sitting on it. Draw curved handlebars and pedals attached to a small circle. Shade the frame (the M shape) with dark to medium colours. Leave a white highlight slightly to one side all the way round the frame. Use a ruler and lightly draw in the spokes. Seen from the front, a bike is like a 'T' with the pedals sticking out slightly.

Boats

Boats are fun to draw but you need to get the proportions right. If you have the chance to look at some boats, notice the negative space around them. A small rowing boat can be drawn with the guideline of a figure 8 on its side. Larger boats, such as yachts have two different sized upright triangular sails.

If you're putting your boat on water, don't draw the base, but add splashes and billows of white to make it appear as if it's moving through the water.

Most boats are made up of a similar shape. They're flat at the back and pointed towards the front. For a speedboat, add a flat box on top of this basic hull shape. If you're drawing an ocean liner, put several smaller boxes on top and add slanted cylinders for funnels.

Drawing from photographs

Photographs can be helpful for all kinds of drawing. They show shapes and tones on a flat surface so you don't need to work things out for yourself how they should look. And you can spend as long as you like drawing from them, knowing that your subject won't move! Animals and birds move around so much and so often, that it's hard to sketch them. With photographs, you can see the shapes of their bodies and the way they move. Photographs give you plenty of detailed information about places that you might never visit and about people you might never meet. Look in magazines, brochures, catalogues and newspapers and collect reference pictures for your sketchbook.

It's fun to sketch from life, but it's not always possible. It might be too cold to sit outside or you might not be stopping in one place for long enough. You might want to finish a portrait and the person might have to move. And what if you want to draw jungle animals or deep-sea creatures? Then photographs - either your own or from magazines - can be very useful. You can use them as a starting point, as a way of learning where and how to draw realistically. You can use bits of one and parts of another to create a whole drawing. Or you can copy them exactly.

But if you use photographs too much, your drawings could easily become lifeless. This happens when photographs become your main source of ideas and your drawings lose originality and seem flat and unimaginative. Counteract this with plenty of drawings from real life and your imagination and some drawings taken from photographs.

DRAWING . . . IS FUN!

Squaring up

When you want to use a small photograph as the basis for a larger drawing, you may find it difficult to copy the photograph in a larger size. By squaring it up, you will keep your picture in proportion.

You will need a sheet of tracing paper. With a ruler, carefully measure equal spaces horizontally and vertically. Draw the grid using the ruler. Then on your paper, draw a larger grid, using the same number of squares. Lay the tracing paper on the photograph and copy the photograph, square by square, on to the paper. This method is easier that straight copying because you can draw each bit as if it's an entire picture.

When you become involved with your drawing, you might become more involved with photography. Armed with a camera as well as a sketchbook, you will be able to sketch as well as snap. When you have your film developed, you will have all the reference you need to produce wonderful, complete drawings with no mistakes!

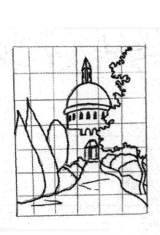

Animals

Animals move about quickly so they can be difficult to draw accurately. If you want to do a detailed drawing of an animal, you'll probably have to use photographs as well. But if you can, try drawing it from life.

Start by capturing the overall proportions and rough shape of the animal. As usual, you need to stop thinking of your idea of what each animal looks like and to look closely at the positive and negative shapes. See how it stands and moves. Many animals' legs bend in the opposite direction to ours. Often paws or hooves aren't set in a straight line on the leg, but tilt forward at an angle.

Horses

As with any animal, to draw a horse you should look at lots of them, from real life or photographs. Get to know parts of their bodies: hocks, fetlocks and mane for instance. Notice the curves of the legs and the back, the shape of the neck and head. The head seems to be made up of two ovals, large at the top and small for the muzzle. Make the stomach curve up slightly towards the back legs and the back legs slope down towards the hocks. Horses' eyes are on either side of the face and slant slightly. The nostrils are wider than ours and the ears point out

DRAWING . . . IS FUN!

from the top of the head. The mane grows down the length of the neck and there should be a shaded line down the length of the neck under the head, indicating the jugular groove. You'll also need to shade in the rounded cheeks.

To draw a horse in action, you need to see the pattern the legs make.

For years, people drew horses running with both sets of legs sticking out front and back, like a rocking horse! After photography was invented, artists took photographs of moving horses and realised that their legs move alternately. From then on, horses were drawn as they really look, with their legs in the right places!

Farmyard animals also make fun subjects. Cows, for instance, are heavier than horses with shorter legs. Their tails look like ropes with a tassel on! Whereas a horse seems to be all curves, a cow has angles at each end of its box-shaped body. A sheep's shape is also a rectangle with rounded ends plus a small wedge-shaped head. It's a good idea to draw the whole animal as a rough outline, rather than becoming stuck on one area and then not getting all the other proportions right.

Shapes, shadow and shine

Once you've got the essential shapes right, start adding texture and tone with soft shading. Leave white streaks to show shine.

Cats and dogs

Drawing dogs and cats is fun - and frustrating! They can sit still for ages then suddenly walk off!

Do some quick studies in your sketchbook. When the animal moves, move on to another sketch. Don't worry if your pictures aren't successful at first. Sketching becomes easier the more you do it.

Cats

Cats are made up of rounded shapes. Their movements are smooth and graceful. They can squash into a ball or stretch into long elegant shapes. Tails grow in a continuous line from their spines. Look for the patterns their legs make when they move. Draw them leaping, climbing, stretching or asleep. Notice how their tails help their balance. Cats' heads are one-third of their height. Draw the face as a circle with an oval in it containing the nose and mouth. The slightly slanted oval eyes 'sit' on this oval with about 1 .5 eyes' gap between them. Kittens' eyes are rounded. Cats' noses are a tiny triangle - very small. Ears are triangular with curved tips. Mouths are small, making an upside-down Y from the nose. Draw spots on either side of the mouth and add a few whiskers. Use shading to show tone and texture, leaving patches of white for the lightest areas.

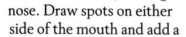

DRAWING . . . IS FUN!

Dogs

Although most dogs are similar, each breed has a different build. Decide which dog to draw and study its shape and proportions. Look at it from the side. What size is the head compared to the body? Do its legs come straight down or do the back legs lean away? How long is the nose? Sketch the rough outline of the entire dog, adding the shape of the legs and tail.

Study all the angles before you sketch them in. The body usually appears wider towards the front legs. The paws can be marked in with circles at the ends of the legs. Look for simple shapes whether you're drawing a sitting, standing or moving dog. Sitting dogs can look a bit like rounded triangles. Standing and moving dogs often appear to be made up of rounded 'sausage-shapes'. Improve the outline and add details later.

Dogs' heads are more box-shaped than cats and their necks are thicker and leaning forward at an angle from the shoulders. What shape is the nose? What about the eyes? Where do the ears come on the head? Shade the darker, undersides of your dog.

You can use all sorts of interesting techniques to show the texture of dogs' and cats' fur. Pastels and charcoal can make a smudgy effect, which is good for all sorts of short fur. Pens can create good effects for longer fur. Pencils can create all types of fur, depending on how you use them.

Draw your pet!

Draw a portrait of your pet for your room! Whether you have a cat, a budgie or a tarantula, your pet is the ideal model because you are familiar with it and you can look at it often. If you don't have your own pet, draw a friend's! Or draw your favourite animal and put that in your room. What about buying a small, inexpensive calendar - just the dates in a little booklet - and glue or staple this on to your finished pet picture? All of these make brilliant presents.

It's always best to draw from a real animal if you can. You can back this up with photographs for detail later. Begin by sketching the pet in lots of positions. Consider the shape, proportions and how you would like to draw the portrait. For instance, will you draw your pet from a sitting, standing or moving position? On the other hand, close-ups are effective. As you have already discovered, pets don't stay still for long, so study different details at different times.

Adding detail

Textures can be shown in several ways. For soft fur, try a soft pencil, such as a 3B. Shade in the direction the fur grows and keep outlines light. Or use coloured pencils and drag a rubber along to lift out highlights. Felt-tips with pastel on top create good fish scales. Coloured pencils with cross-hatching on top make effective reptile skin. Make dark areas darker than you think they should be and if you're using colour, add blue or purple for shadows rather than black. Be light in touch and don't let colours mix and become muddy. Rabbits, guinea-pigs, mice, gerbils and hamsters are soft and rounded. They look good drawn in pencil or pastels on tinted paper. Add some whiskers. Leave a tiny white highlight on their little black eyes.

Only smudge with your fingers when you use pastels. Everything else should be smudged with pressure of the pencil, pen or crayon only.

Make eyes look shiny. This is in contrast with most pets' skin covering. So after you've made smudgy, furry marks for fur, patterned fish scales, or wispy feathers, shade the eyes using strong contrasts - black for the pupil and a white highlight spot.

As with all drawings, don't just draw a symbol of what you imagine your pet looks like. For example, rabbits' tails are not little round powder puffs on their bottoms! They're furry ovals that tip upwards.

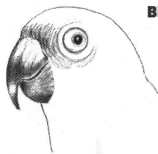

Birds

Birds have rounded, streamlined shapes. They're sort of egg shapes with tail feathers. Their heads form a point with their beaks. Their wings are attached to their spines, so they come out of the top of the body, not the sides.

You can do it!

Now you're well on your way to being a great artist. Remember that there are no real rules about what makes a good drawing, so try not to be too critical of your work. Be bold and experiment with materials and styles. Good drawings can be the result of hours' hard work or a few minutes' quick sketch.

Presentation

When you've completed a drawing, keep it clean and flat. If you've used chalk pastels or charcoal, spray the picture lightly with fixative (or cheap hairspray which is just as effective). Always spray near an open window.

For finished drawings, not in your sketchbook, cut frames from stiff card. Measure the size you want with a ruler and cut it out carefully with a craft knife or scissors. Back the picture with a sheet of card as well. When you have several drawings, give your own art exhibition for family and friends!

Or back the picture on to larger sheets of card and make greetings' cards. Using a photocopier and colouring pencils you could produce several versions in different colours. Experienced artists draw all the time. It's how they keep their work fresh and interesting. You can do all the exercises in this book in different subjects and styles. The only limit is your imagination.

So good luck with your drawing, but most of all - *have fun!*

DRAWING . . . IS FUN!

You've reached the end of this book and discovered that
Drawing . . . Is Fun!
So how are your writing skills? What better way to use your
drawings than with your own story, poem or magazine!

Writing is more than just schoolwork, it can be great fun - an exciting and rewarding hobby or even a career! Enter the world of storytelling - bound only by your imagination. Find out what it's like to be a super-hero (or a super-model) and write about it - with yourself in the starring role! Or get out your notebook and become a reporter - you can even start your own magazine. Gordon Wells shows you how to develop your skills and produce great results:
Create real, talking characters
Write a great poem
Organise and present your writing for greatest effect.

ISBN 1-902713-03-6

And lots more - you'll be amazed at how quickly you improve once you start. Whatever your interests, fashion and football or animals and the environment, express your best ideas in writing and impress your friends, family, teachers - and, most of all, yourself!

Writing . . . Is Fun! is available at £4.99 and you can order direct from Writers' Bookshop! Just call 01733 898103 or write to Writers' Bookshop, Remus House, Coltsfoot Drive, Woodston, Peterborough PE2 9JX.
Alternatively, pop into your local bookshop!